SUN OF CONSCIOUSNESS

Édouard Glissant

Sun of Consciousness

Translated by Nathanaël

Nightboat Books

Copyright © 1997 Editions GALLIMARD, Paris
English Translation Copyright © 2020 by Nathanaël
Published originally as *Soleil de la conscience: Poetique I* by Éditions Falaize in 1956

ISBN: 978-1-93765-895-3

This translation was carried out with the aid of a fellowship from the Centre National du Livre de France and with the support of the Terre d'Arts collective in conjunction with ETC Caraïbe (Martinique).

Cover design and interior typesetting by Kit Schluter
Text set in EB Garamond

Cataloging-in-publication data is available from the Library of Congress

Nightboat Books
New York
www.nightboat.org

to Maurice Aliker
Prisca Jean-Marie
and Laurent Ortolé

FROM THE GAZE TO LANGUAGE

Winter has its redoubtable seductions, from which safeguard is sometimes necessary... Having come from Martinique (which is an island of the Caribbean circle) and living in Paris, I have been here for eight years engaged in a French solution: I mean that it is not only so because it is so decided on the first page of a passport, nor because it happens that this language and this culture were taught to me, but indeed because I feel a growing necessity in a reality from which I cannot abstain. A very individual case that none, to various ends, could utilize toward a more general orientation. This French culture, in which by turns I observe its most extreme measure, its most precious concern for the order of art, and on the contrary its unlimited disturbance, its naked revelation, suggests its most maritime movement to me, with such little monotony. But am I able to say, in detail, that I feel Racine, for example or the Cathédrale de Chartres? Sensitive to the swaying, to the swell of waves, may I buoy in some hollow of the tide, take pleasure or live there really? I let my gaze wander, from this time that I said, over these landscapes of French knowledge. Not like the voyager who only expects from the monuments' appearance the receipt for his departure; but like such a one as would domesticate the doubt of knowing. I divine perhaps that there will be no more culture without all of the cultures, no one civilization that can be the metropole to the others, nor a single poet to ignore the movement of History. And already, inscribed in the effort that is particular to me, I can no longer deny this evidence, which is best accounted for in an imaged manner: which is that here, by a very homogeneous and reasonable enlargement, are literally imposed upon my eyes the gaze of the son and the vision of the Stranger.

Paris, when falling in (for me it was through the gray hole of the Gare Saint-Lazare) scarcely astonishes: so much have the arts of reproduction, the monolithic obstinacies of Education or the imagination rife in books accustomed you to entering. To begin with, one declines, scarcely touched: "Really, that was all..." Paris closes very quickly over the newcomer, and for a fairly long deferment, the vast overtures that each had in himself and from a distance prepared, relocated. This city refuses itself as much as it is denied, I want to say in its beginnings. In these parts there is the peculiarity of a Free-Masonry, a necessity, at all times disconcerting, for a rite of initiation, which in the very air solicits attention and irritates. Each finds himself in his room; and how this situation (the very expression) leads to the thought of the insular or the tropical. Behold, backhanded exoticism. It must be taken up. But already, friends have come, the slow cadence of seasons seizes being with a new rhythm. Then, by a sort of obscure secretion, the consciousness of the rhythm that comes to signify rhythm comes to light. For the periodic return of winter and summer is very particular to teaching Measure. In other words, vertiginously, to accelerate this work of consciousness which animates all savoir-vivre. Now the very flash of life turns around and illuminates itself at length;

Measure is of knowledge. (Is there not loss of life, deviation, smothering, at that sole moment at which Measure is made into the very matter upon which it must only be exerted?) Man, from frosts to harvests, wants to measure his sun, like the priest of a religion of stars. In this quest, each frustration competes, and all plenitudes as well.

Nowhere as much as here is the privilege of talent granted, after a toll. A sort of frenzy in the consumption of works (this was especially true in the years 1946, 1947, 1948). But who would have the imprudence to claim, without having a "name" already, that art, or the study of an art, signify for him the ambition of a knowledge? Don't go confiding that you are struggling, that you are searching, that this business is close to your heart. Paris doesn't like gravity that appears as affectation. A manner of detachment (which isn't even discretion) gives an impression of "lucidity." Leave it to others to discover in your work "its deep resonances...," and offer in appearances only ease. The too obvious search for essence is a mark here of weakness, instead of worried casualness. Ideas that risk being too easily received, because they are "in the air," each keeps from offering them up raw. Here we are at the opposite of collective literatures, of legends a thousand times known but always heeded, of fervors around texts, of vigils of an entire people near the storyteller, of the acceptation of the word as a commonplace for all: of what made literatures the living weapon, felt to be alive, of civilizations. Paris plays at literature, at art. Yet, in the cellars of this Museum, what veritable fervor does the city not consume? A gripping image of a culture still vital and already ablaze with crisis.

The bit of security that allows for the belief in work and keeps pure the night around the lanterns, let it not run dry: I don't dare rise yet. The high cliffs that ever you carry inside you, open them for a Word, open a dawn in the rock. And all these years whose face is fury, the words of yesterday amass there! I fear hastening this night. Exhausting already this night in which darkness rises like a deceased lover. I am stubborn with this ultimate clarity of before morning: it is savage and dense, some splendor that is starved for itself: a treasure of Low Vegetations...

Pale rain, solitude, the droughts of late scarcely, already you are grazing at our very ancient wounds. I hunt you, and it is this frizzy will to hold on to this night, to come to life with a Surge now more beautiful than when it goes into the forest vested for the future snow; to cry at last in the full fire of Fire, I who am laughing in all this marble — marble being the lyric newness of trees when winter enters the heart and unpeoples it...

So I push some islands against the wall, I isolate a swath of silence and unleash it. Then I pick up the earth that has fallen, the earth of experience, word by word, with the effort. An impatience cracks, but I am waiting for the chirrup of the eye to illuminate the depths: the gasping of High Vegetations among the night now free to follow its course, I won't hold it back! All of the past in this drop of rain presses and jostles the coming day...

It is clear that poetry is out of balance here, and that together I am tending to engage it, unable to do otherwise. Yet this major difficulty is still of meaning and of the governance of prose. What I would first like to establish is the quasi-necessity for a chaos of writing at a time in which being is all chaos; in other words how expression follows the same blueprint as the individual. But why, and when, would being be all chaos. When, for example, feeling as though thrown into a very collective adventure, at the beginning of some new journey, dazzled he frolics, tempted by a thousand successive directions, before finding his order. If it happens moreover that this being is deported, physically deported from his center of adventure, the imbalance is accentuated, but in the same time the recovery of self accelerates.

Yet in the Antilles, where I come from, it can be said that a people constructs itself positively. Born of a culture medium, in this laboratory where each table is an island, here is a synthesis of races, of mores, of knowledges, but which tends toward its own unity. Can this synthesis, such is effectively the question, achieve unity? Will it be possible to observe, now that these problems are of interest to the human sciences, observe in the flesh the work of a being stirring himself, and being borne of his own will (clay that allocates, without a demiurge, its own breath?) This question that my existence asks of me, it could be said, inasmuch as I am already replying, that it poses me as being: so am I the ethnologist of myself. A question that was not without dramatic echoes, rendings or bewilderments, across the ages: how, in effect, could the work of synthesis and the conquest of unity not have necessitated labor (in judgments, fixations, betrayals, sectarianisms, imbecilities, caste laws...) of those who were simultaneously object and subject? To be born to the world is an exhausting splendor. And for whomever wishes to guard the testimony of this birth, there is a time of chaotic opening, of anarchic presentiment of history, of furious masticating of words, of vertiginous seizure of clarities which, though born to oneself, one is tossed to the handsome forefront of the world. But I will return to this further: prose, chaos, measure, knowledge and poetry being signs of my experience, seen from inside. Outside, it is the French truth opposing mine; by this revealed alliance of an opposite to its other, in which it is known that all truth is its dialectical consummation.

The plain, interminable; Europe. Practise at recognizing changes in landscapes, where the eye had initially formulated only an exhausting flat surface. Then, the Mediterranean. Never, never before had the thought of the cold been associated for me with the thought of the sea. The sea was the opposite of winter, just as the mountain was its homonym. I am told the Atlantic is ever more icy, on the coasts of Bretagne and Normandie for example; it hadn't occurred to me upon arrival at Le Hâvre. Diverting inventory of the shivering salting. Leaving, I climb northward to the still fields. Shifting wheat, never tousled by the drunken ascent of a comb, like the nourishing canna of snakes. This infinite tile of lands imprisons me. Far from the window of the train, I think of the electric speech of flame trees, that from afar pilots still believe to be sheets of blood — left on the sidelines of crime...

I am taking up this experience of the snow again. For a long time, from over there, I surmised it, threatening beauty. And the first time it offered its foam to my eyes, it was just like a rain. I had known it before. Better yet, it broke the grayness to confer at last to winter the only splendor of its word. So it advances the real image of the cold season, its prefigured essence: it delivers from expectation and luminously it contradicts, it is almost hot. Such is the snow to me: an illumination (I am finally touching winter), an opening (I am finally at one with this spectacle), the enlargement, the established communication (snow: as singular, durable, definitive as the heavy sun), the power now to accelerate the dialogue, to hold close its common reasons, as at the fireside. With it I come out of indecision to be carried to the extreme opposite of my order. It seems that the whole way is travelled, and that now understanding is all that is required. Elementary wager of my new disposition to garner. Here I am making it into my delights but so naturally. Truly, try as I might, I cannot know the exotic call of the new that I have so often observed in the bearing of our sandalled visitors. What are nonetheless this lack, this wasting I must evade — if not the sign that every being arrives at the consciousness of the world through his own world first; as universal (to speak broadly) as much as he is individual; as generous and common that he was able to become alone, and inversely?

I like these fields, their order, their patience; nonetheless I do not partake of them. Having never disposed of my land, I haven't at all this atavism of the economy of land, its organization. My landscape is a temper yet; the symmetry of plantings hinders me. My time is not a succession of seasonal hopes, it is still of surges and breaches of trees. When I will truly possess my land, I will organize it according to my order of clarities, according to my learned time. This means that the quest for the free wind (the apprenticeship of the earth) is chaos and immoderation, frenzied landscape, forest without a converted clearing; but that it is Measure (labor, sowing, harvests) that is freedom. Every rotting civilization first loses its sense of Measure, either by submitting it to an unfounded disorder, or on the contrary by stuffing and statufying it. So is knowledge of liberated matter that turns against itself, examines and orders itself — without nonetheless abutting in a catalogue of fixed forms. And out of the chaos that had first to be lived in order to be endured, here we alight in a summer of pure vigils. What, if not building? Constructing and testing oneself? All poetry that, in its deepest structures, stimulates Measure, I do mean according to organic exigencies, and not out of formal affectation or coquetry, is liberty.

Here you are in a workday like a laborer, watching, under the ploughshare, for the lips of the earth — *(... again I see the House of the Sea. In the last turn of the last grain of the last beach, my voice, and against it the malefic daughters of distance. A child alone with at her neck and her sleeves the constellations of desire... Then, the Heights: a path on the morne heckles, the adjutant bulls battle for the most beautiful, and her name is: Générale ("Oh Générale Oh")... Black cowherds augur tempests of knowledge...)* — And in a day of laziness you are as though in the condensed richness of a greenhouse, a tree benefitting. Memories, your work is not fecund, you only have material, your truth is founded upon sadness only; elsewhere, I gather joy and a dawn. From the elucidation of chaos to the illustration of measure, there is a long distance that is created at the outset by the slow approach of knowledge and then the dull tasking of suffering. The poem after the poem paves with momentary acquisitions these itineraries that each conducts in himself to learn for ever.

Poem (1948)

*And the oar is of earth in the expectation of the new country
Oceania and the love of you is a tissue atop a mast Oceania the
love of you a coconut tree of mists in your presence Oceania in
your smile of cathedrals devoted to no worship and I tame the
foam of your dresses and Asia and Europe in our childhoods
Asia is a polyparium that inhabits itself and gnaws at itself
between sky and battle and for it Europe is a field of nails. To
no longer hear the unreal retting of the wild butterflies of the
dense day. Many and more are the elections of assassins in the
beautiful cancerous rain. Oh the most beautiful earth in which
to perfect the lactescence of our harvests oh the most beautiful
in which to amass our skins and upon them the perdurition of
clouds the most beautiful oh fingers of the liana of undergrowth
in the ringing desert bell, Africa. The last mission was to set
the word astray in the teeming deafness, burnt Tropic. Like a
sum of fruits drunk with remembrances in the mute desire of
banana plants.*

Strange nuptials of the earth and of the heart, under the sign and the surge of the sovereign sea. For here, on this island, the encircling that risked hindering the imagination, on the contrary exacerbates and rushes upon it, maritime breakaways. So the roundabout is consummated, the man falls and embraces the earth. The lit waves are dizzying, the air ferments and raises him up, but the earth is in him like an ineffaceable suffering. He has drawn from the strange and tortured his laugh. Closed, surrounded, burning to imagine the rest in his image, he must open, he must open himself, see otherwise, the other. After which, behind each grin there is a dawn. From one horizon to the other such a deep ardor of his drunken voice sustains him. He has no interest in strolls, exaltations, the flames of setting suns. This ardor is so secret, intimate, so known. It ignites an orchard, fired fruits, of acrimony or sweetness, in turn: so is the poem born. The island is a shard in lightning, that the tree everywhere conducts inwardly.

I remember the story of the woman who for a whole night was suckled by a serpent, without daring to move. Terrible silence and congealment. I hate the serpent avid for milk! (But this cannot be a poem that I would here devastate from West to East. Because a poem is a breaker of waves, lap of lands and then, a poem does not allow itself to be led and pillaged by will power or summation of being. This is the wave's advance after a hill as well as a beat of blood; and the blood spurts in the earth and at the ten chapped fingers of recollection, not in the machine of the heart. The night is seen advancing like a procession of dews, the smirking night. Ah! the odor of the fetish-tree, rotten, crawling all the way to the city... but thought never peels its astonished face of torture!) Now I speak the horror and the madness — that harnessing all night long of a serpent to the breast of a statufied woman.

Your drupes turn, your milk turns, you howl in the icy splendor of terror, inside of silence — but above all you do not move! To feel the venomous wilt ravage the flesh, the childhood of your strength, the milk, more surely than a thousand years of black ordeal; this panting of a beast in you who bathes, and it could kill you with a sudden blow, but no (the serpent is intelligent) it prefers to astound you with horror, and calmly drinks. Do you separate from this suddenly assailed woman the earth that beneath her shudders? Do you make one of her milk and two of the earthy milk of earth without their ever espousing one another? I make of this earth the face of every woman raped in her tender milk: of this woman the image of every earth shaken so that her milk will weep, as from a prune tree.

(I do not know how to describe, inch upon inch describe each bird's eyelid raised by the cries of morning, nor the misery, the death of the lights in the eyeless shacks — but I know order, the scattering. Therefore this is not at all the book of suctions, as that of a cleric, but still the order according to which the future fructified, that is of savors under the peel. All the gathered children, all the flowering clays are the rearing of this tomorrow.)

And when a serpent suckles a motionless woman, he speaks to her silently, in other words in his sucking language: "Do not complain, I bring you the sense and the glory of my order, the perfect circle." Shaken, silently as well, she redrew in her poor capsized head the voyage of her body. Shoulders where love ripens as well as guava, mad bolt of the horses of August. Hips in which the whole day in vain sought out the day to separate from laziness its toil — and nothing was chaff: not the grave accomplishment of sleep, nor at the outskirts the humid range of furrows. She mourned her body. And an invasion of furors germinated already from her night...

So from the distance of writing does one see nothing more on the plain than a crumpling of lands. The memory is narrow in which a tent must then be raised. Beware, you are alone in this drama. Exceed the silk of your breath, cross the barrier of your hands, but upon return be of silence. Recharge your solitude and pensive, climb your steps. Your night? In your heavy night behold morning grows, its high leaves that are struggle. Between two pumps of milk, you don't know anymore whether you are acquiescing or whether you are biting down. Struggle: a fascination, as regards the stiff head, and the vivacious body in revolt (as regards the bosom) and withdraws already. From this night (from this struggle) to this beauty, the way will be natural.

And you, I defy you by fire and by the moving forest in your heart to forever spell this edict of grace upon us, in your heart, by our worries more beautiful than stars, without weeping.

Here we are then several of us very new in the all-power of History. And History is that roused monster to which we cannot deny a tribute. It has imprisoned man that made it, in other words it returns him to the duties for which he is truly incumbent: so Saul of Tarsus claimed to be imprisoned in Jesus Christ. There are those who charged History with clarity. There are those who explored its beauty. The time will come when its knowledge will be accomplished, sufficiently at least to allocate new forms to sensibility: by naming finally the sparse possibilities for expression in the Domain of the Past and of the Future, open henceforth onto the Present.

But is it not already so? Did not Europe experience to satiety that sovereign splendor that deported her to other skies? Did she not, thirsting, learn the extent of the bursting of her eternity? Did she not keep a log of her travels, from Paris to Jerusalem, from the ices of Canada to the rocks of Tierra del Fuego? Now, assemble the lands. A fire of air solicits each word of the work. Beauty, vagabond of the universe, attempts to equal herself in eternal movement: she, fleeting but explored.

Those who are the sons of History, who have come from the world, and feel themselves immoderate! When they measure themselves against History itself, knowledge places in them its rigid liberty.

But Expression, the entire diffuse force of the world is powerless, as long as it has not, this force, been concretely tried. I say that the event, this transport from one shore to another, by which this force tries itself, is only expressible, adorned for offering, through and after the silence that succeeds it. Nocturnal truth. The entire diffuse force of the world is powerless in Expression, if you have not swum from this shore to this other one, then enriched your silence on the new strand. Imagination is shared, can only sustain a common surge; it is nonetheless a tributary of silence, which is individual. And the diffuse force, each can fix, but it must stem from a generosity of all. And the common surge, each can sustain, but after having realised in himself, the concrete force, one here and now; after having thrust into the event then traversed the silence. Yes the individual is disunited for being radically spared the commons; and the imagination: its most self-evident power, historically already, is to enrich in each the will of all, and of all things...

I am back from the land of death. Stars, indistinct places. There, each truth is condemned to start over against the alimentary earth, its question. It was raining on each thing; distant, the ardor of writing, of formulating. The chorus disunited, I walked in the encumbrage of night. Each truth, profuse, flush with the ground like a discreet darnel, perpetuated its bramble. Why the need to retrace one's steps, sounding the bruised bodies of young plants at a verge. Cultivating this darnel is for us a fatality. Yet, from the Event to the Expression, what is the margin (so I asked all day long)? The first propels you into that limitless field where the cry is a retreat, and a reset. You are made to drink all the tears of the earth. The other recaptures you from down belowest, and it is the voyage of the word that reforms. How? — everything has passed. Where do they meet? Listen to the silence: place is, in and upon the imagination, the assumed ill of all. My event, did I say so, was of the uninhabitable and of the quest, the other each time unpeopled...

There is also waiting, a cool chamber among the trees. It is an afternoon of remembrance, when the alleys are populated, provided one pays attention, with promises of shadows and steps; or the serene application of a thought to the flight of water, close by. Behold a river everywhere fordable; scarcely does it rack, three steps wide, the now-overheated prairie. A crow is patient there, ripening what impossible flights: furious, white, shimmering? He has nailed this minute, with motionless presence. Butterflies of heat. Vanquished time. Waiting. The latter carries the body of what is speakable, we surround it with words that gently shine. When the word grows, waiting is replete, and the event achieves its fire. Light, so you splash; Things that move, your life under the hand immortalizes, becomes fixed; alone Immobile, finally are you not here?...

I spoke the struggle of bulls on the mornes. To gather the beasts scattered on the slope — they answered to the names of *Soldat, Chinois, Générale, Souris, Étoile...* — the cowherds deployed a large red drape, and shrieked so as to overcome the herd, which rushed up finally to plough this sheet of blood.

See those grayish slopes, the denuded rocks; nail upon them a sun mad with its own heat. The males quarrel furiously over a female. The entirety hurtle down toward the paddock. Dusts and drool. For me, everything was red, anger, formless cavalcade, so long. Then the moment came, of silence and waiting.

All the force, these revelations, these visions, this fire at last, what is it? The rebirth of a common will, its course in each. And the Form (for if this force is matter, it goes toward that other, the word), we see at once that it is scarcely primary, is but the accomplished electricity of two repellent matters, that the art of man forces to be joined. All the diffuse force can do nothing without Expression, which is second. What is Revelation, without the device and ornament of the right word? A shadow without a guardian, a body without clarity.

But behold expectation and silence have accomplished their office. I go down in this water, memory alone and yet so real, the sea. Sign of what is pure, and I had one day to return to that purity, whatever the cost, in order to praise it. Because light is the purity of water! But I say it still: a bonce of clay suffices for me, red clay and opaque, with its surrounding sky.

Power of the winter that organizes. It is that wound in the day by which the white night penetrates. Its office is to force each toward his own weightedness. Winter stalks memory. You whiten, fingers clumsy. The sky is a blued casting, stacked houses where the smile is all-intimate, and where hope, a prisoner, bivouacs. Passer-by, stirrer, hoarsened on so many beds of frost, your breath measures the talent of the illustrator of shadows. In you, there is very little dawn. Yet you need only unchain the words of the childhood that survives itself. This language. What does language matter then, I mean if it was taught to you or whether you knew it firstly? What does atavism matter, the supple science of diction? *The city is all the more secret that you offer yourself to its secret; the Measure will be the same for all; yet whosoever seeks unity first crystalizes it in his own language.* And this language disproportions a new language, awkward certainly, that wants to bite. Then it slows, fulfills itself and circulates, on the black roads, at the bedside of the other moons.

THE COURSE OF THE POEM

Each time that over the city morning reappears, the silence of nascent clarity presses gently on the body and inspires a scrutiny akin to a prayer. I cannot extinguish the lamp, I wouldn't see a word; yet its light is already too white. In the clear of the room — clear of dawn and clear of night-light — the mind is whetted, aggressive. But just as the electric firefly is extinguished in the day, without nonetheless dying; also does the critic blunt, lose himself sadly in the pleasure, which is not without retreat, of reading.

The poem offers to the reader a space that satisfies his desire to move, to exit himself, to travel by a new land, where he will nonetheless not feel himself a stranger. If the work is "good," one breathes in it, benefits from it; if the work is "bad," all movement within it is impossible for the reader. Such is the critical exercise by which, consulting the poet's universe, at the same time I experience my universe, that I feel (or do not feel) to be in solidarity with his own.

This work of morning cannot be undertaken on the very labor of the worker. Unless the time has passed during which the individual has become the other, who will confront his current universe with his defunct universe. I am resolved: and from this moment on I push away any savor at all, inherent to the poem, flesh of its flesh. It is nothing more than the blueprint of a movement, a stippling of milestones on the path of the course. I abandon the selfish frequenting of the poem, and, overflying it, I fasten it to such and then to such other: whence, this line of force. Perhaps then may I reignite the fires, understand what each morning the naked silence of the dew suggests, and that it will be necessary, on this day again, to continue or perfect.

Bursts of wind: everyone dreams, as a child, of the Only Poem. To be a poet, to become one, is perhaps to exhaust this dream, to have it denied. It is to warrant an eternal lack, that of knowledge. For which the poet, that stranger, is in effect through his poem the known in its totality, its very bearing. This ancient dreamer despairs, he has once and for all despaired of knowing. It is said that he raises the voices of the impossible, without a wish, for himself, to be spared; but his lack of appetition is still joy of tempter. And the headstrong labor only leaves in manners of residue, besides so many draughts, an eternally recommenced homage to art. But art is not, if it can be said and if anyone can yet say so, the end of poetry: artistic success being but the sign of what has been approached again and again. What approached? Such revealing unity of the world, and its absolute, which is the chimera of the mind. Poets cease forthwith to consider a single poem, good or bad, to establish themselves on the contrary in a sort of duration. Also, when the time has come for the New Reason, to give ancient texts to read, the first for example that were actually ever written, is to have the courage (being sure of nothing yet) to return to those initial pages to attempt to lay bare the motives, the dream of origins. How the approach of knowledge is precisely artistic accomplishment, and vice versa, remains to be shown. But this is of another toil... Proceeding further, it can already be proposed that the scattered poem, which more than a draught is nearly the floatation line between two completed poems, can be just as essential if not durable. At least could its testimony be so inferred, in other words the ambition signaled by its very imperfection, if there were nary any completed poems? For, it's all the same: the same fire.

Primary chaos. What is experience is derisory as long as it has not been corrected by thought. Man cries out his volcano, he compiles lava upon lava. Ungainly, he suggests, and struggles among the nonetheless distant proofs. He abstracts and renders general the concrete forces: he wrings and blanches them. I was populating that Parisian solitude, I was trying to nail solar keys to the measured door of the New Domain. And I gave over to what was elemental...

Elements (1949)

Oh extinguished suns! I will regain a health of fruits aflame! and also... rasping with his only tooth (of storm of blood of tear) the big lick of acceptance... A jaw of sands of deserts, and may the other be of asters dawns pollens: let him set the stars and broken necks the whip the master who sepulchers and the stalks of cane whistling waiting and the pain and the blood, his poetry and his racket of poetry... Akin, without repute filigreeing unheard of tropical stages, to the black lick beneath the wind!

Listen,
leaning on silence, to the elephant trumpeting.

My braided house defiant of lightning, of reeds flown from October's hougans, my house my house of marine crystal long wall of America. The rebel blacklisted for teaching children that the hand has but one finger. I stir the bracken of waves. My wakening is of dog dragging his kennel under bridges.

Errance caught in a trap, obsolete
when when and when the unfleshed
bells of the inaudible?

Yet I am in History that monster to the slightest marrow of elder. Secularly settled, but strong like ignorance. I await (voration of the poem) the roses. Blacks not killed incinerated decapitated but lynched. I circulate among the coals. My force flattened against the forces!

(Amusers, and here they are rising! A fine scandal! Here in the name of poetic demarking, and to testify for moral splendor. I oblige myself thereupon to salute: man, that luminous desire for song. Vocative, excess...)

The forest suddenly howls to life. The stars, prowlers, invade the locks! Alive oh alive, queen. Your feet go the way, abandoned mango trees. Your peeled skin is a grandiose red labor. Alive

oh alive my prairie morning you my prairie night raped at the bullfight. You slid into the water the gasping of your silhouette cut with glass. At the ford the black beach the black sand of caresses. In the aster handsome aster of your hands. Tranquil round-up of dawns in the blazing nave of your dreams, and your voice of proclaimed splendor, of darnel mixed with darnel: I suspend the storm at the wayside altar of your lips!

Ah suddenly
the fear of being two
in beauty!

the flash of you the mane of snows; the flash of you air and love interlaced. You snaking and labored. Me foam of your step...

I was rebellious as a colony of child martyrs of found dogs of unconverted sharks! O suffering, that wind beating in the streets. And poverty is ignorance of the earth, the imagination is passion. But no crackling, no sun, since the open mouth of man alone awaits!

Oh tremulated stone!

Man plundered-alive, labor

Maculated storm oh

for you I am blood, marvelous chalice! Roots, roots, I will never have done pulling on your fertile dugs! The fire chooses this wave that I took to be the last, to encircle me in turn.

It was furious rush of the herds. Out of this sequence of (sincere...) cries what teaching could emerge? Chaos to part with. Gangue, without the diamond. Revelation, without ornament. No contradiction with this which, beyond this moment of wild torrent, the individual (the lost man), yet misjudges the law of the poem, and, pressed as he is to be at last in the "right," attempts to lead in it,

either an impalpable song (a song of remembrance!) — in which a need for order rages, which amounts only to the lure of a device of convention:

1949

We follow you enraptured
bird-trappers of noon, bird-trappers
we follow you, a long way

All foams closed
Upon your renewed eyes
Singing will be your heart

And upon your hands of glimmers
The earth is, oh bird-trappers
Of noon, a road so red —

or a burn of Ancient Times (the nostalgia for the "golden age," or more simply the first age):

1953

Desperate, heart of joy
On the sand, emotion of your days,
That an earth be the chalice,

Oh Mounts and Swells, cold laws
Of the riches that are in us
Rivers betrayed by your shores

On the face of the deaf sea
Did you recognize my friends? —

or the very theoretical (and what's more, vague) programming of desires:

1953

The tree flowered with words
He wrote at morning
The wind gave him reply.
The path had not moved
The knowledge was elsewhere;
Oh beneath the word there is a fruit
In which are sleeping at last those who know
Their sleep to be innocent.
Such who is tree has no wind
Such who sleeps forgets the path...

Such is the tensing of language, which is sometimes mistaken for the truth of one's profound order. Thus is it possible to believe that the Alexandrine is but a line of twelve feet which hangs a rhyme in the balance; but its true sense is beyond its number or the vocalizations of the last syllable. When the matter of the Alexandrine (twelve feet, one rhyme) is made into the measure of this line, then it is betrayed. And this is the currency of my subject: to find the just measure of my primordial chaos. In which I failed repeatedly, for having mistaken the organic rule toward which I tender, for an icy slowing or stuffing. (Yes, here I do engage poetry: that it grant me the signification of my language, to testify to the signification of my history. That it accomplish through me its work, to thereby illustrate the work of my consciousness seizing me). Winter, you ice the voice. That is why I am still seeking, glory to you, the clear diction of this rhythm, a savoir-vivre.

Poetry tempts the scale of the emotions of the world, the reset of infinite material confidence when man is capable of stealing several of its echoes. What is offered here is the seizure of a tenebrated myriad, the brilliance of which, in order to be perceived, demands the nudity of the spectator: his nudity his offering. But beneath the myriad each day does the armature thicken whose splinters are meat. Each day man discovers and feels a new bone in his skeleton. Behold, from the splinter of the instant to the armature of duration, the poetic knowledge that scours its space, concentrated at the peak of the poem. It abandons itself at the surface, this knowledge, to the myriad; and in depth imposes itself upon the texture. With one same movement forsakes to impose itself, imposes to forsake itself again, motionless sea and in tides toward the myriad and its armor. Here (in the flash of appearance) it is embrasement, spark of the present that freezes in the word; it is measure and patience, there, (underneath), dull duration, sufferance and joy, new reason that makes the weft between words, and animates the frost. No art as much as poetry is bound to the apocalyptic course of human knowledges. No art has this much need to be at the extreme vigil of knowledge. No art can be more summoned to open upon man this reason for all things, which will sublimate reason. So does man run to encounter the world; and rids himself in due course, as of a pointless burden, of the weight of his being. But he must have himself in order to reject himself! Still, does he not already know that at the last, in the marriage and the always recommended scholarship that finish the course (for it to take up again), it is himself he will retrieve: commonplace of the rupture that spatters and of the measure that reunites?

The voyager returns to the burden of roots, and deliberates as to the waters of the delta. There is, each morning of speaking, like a caressing austerity of words; the earth, with its accidents of flesh, takes the shape of harvest. Duration of knowledge, is patience, obscure stirring, argillaceous obole: the Song.

(In this sloughing blaze is an island, where each provision will be kept.)

Like movement, recognizing itself in its very flight, the island, which is secret, is accomplished in its radiance. Diamond of contraries also, the voice of man borrows from all tones and is concentrated in its gravity, opening nonetheless to its diversity. In the illusory deregulation, the number finally establishes a severity. The eternal search is the sole eternity of the true, as of the beautiful which is its vestment. That is there is no point of eternity which is not malleable. The island is passing, its provision remains.

But always, burning the throat, there is a sort of unaccomplished necessity! I write out of my house, terrible vacancy! I fulfill this expanse between joy and the threshold. And waiting, I amplify the wait with the lives that are aroused but that also once were. When everything stops, I stop too, I remain there in the noise of the passersby. I write far from my house, to return to it safe, to gain its concrete flesh, distance...

If you suffer without weakness the star of snow and its pressure on your body, then your eyes open to the sunlit space of memory. I await the plenitude of the word that is given. I do not seek within it, knowing that to search it is here to impoverish it. I dig nearby. And the House opens onto the brilliance of the word. Now, I cross the Atlantic again. Either, in effect, that this ship with its seemingly virgin name of earth, Colombia, will carry me off; or, straying not from its gray stone, that I will find a voice again and begin the dialogue throughout Paris. Now, I do not go onto the Mountain — wait, wait; the Sea grows by me.

I write at last near the Sea, in my burning house, on the volcanic sand.

THE TWO PAGES OF THE VOYAGE

I cry out at first:

Go to the cities, purify the silence of stones — here is the obscure and the reunited. This is for scholarship. For instinct, we have measured it! Man redresses his disaster, he adorns it! *And this scholarship of our wanting! It is verge, here it is perhaps...*

(and this is how I address the clouds of kayali, fugitive birds, so fearful of salt, and deliberate in the azure of leaving.)

Then I evoke:

So, after the high volcanic spectacles, the calamitous embraces of the Pelees — forgotten, torrid death, and the pillagers of wrecks have fed their blood with this cinder — the lava cools upon its summer, it does not suffer the voice's affliction nor the hand's admiration. These wounded statues, surging from what entrail, remain gray. Their word astonishes. But the agony of their venules, beside themselves, illumine the fleet of birds. Oh Death. May an overture carry away this sand! And may the wind, in its outburst, be again as a river of summers...

(it is that I am now in the confidence of the cobbles, which are expansed lava.)

THE EXPERIENCE REVEALED

Left the tragic joy of the House, and have taken up the course of snows again. This experience of Europe took, as can be said of a vaccine; and I may no longer retract. But to evoke it, is to know it. And this knowledge (which intervenes after the unfolding, after the trial) is, alone, free of choice. It introduces the subject-object into the realm of its future discoveries. A trial, yes; from which it was not given to me to subtract myself. But a knowledge, yes; and beforehand I did not know that it was possible to catch up so naturally with the course. As though, in any case, the place had been marked: the place in crisis specifically, in the moment of crisis specifically; and only there could it be marked.

I have said the chaos of writing in the surge of the poem. I will say it now in the draught of prose. Just as I knew that it was not enough for a poem to be borne away by a wind of immoderation for it to accomplish in a durable manner the summer of a being, however disproportionate; I similarly glimpsed at last that prose gives order to that which is otherwise given. But well before, I was hacking up pages of prose, not even able to console myself with thinking that I was making them unbeknownst, persevering nonetheless, accepting that I was tempted. As with those people who have done you harm and who then want to help you, to make up for themselves, or because this way they feel themselves clear of the harm they have done you — assistance, favors, good that you receive, because you cannot but. So, in the solitude stirred from inside failure, I persuaded myself that one day I would manage to say, heavily, what was set upon my heart. Without knowing that my inability originated, yes, from the fact that the experience was not replete. That the word of the first day is epileptic, skates over its own surface. That this seething subsides, when out of the void of death and the irremissible matrix, will surface the knowledge of the matrix and of the death that reduces them at the last, and is birth. Knowledge that is not decline, that is not the confounding of taxidermy with the real order. Without knowing also that the heights of experience unleash ordinance (the harvest); that I would finally try to rally the beginning and the end. Without even knowing that experience was from the mirror of this old continent, on its silvering of panes and of solitude, where my image appears to me: such as I feel it, but such also as it is felt by those whom I finally look at in turn.

Racism must be spoken of. Here, everything is nuances; I therefore now accuse what is more of an impediment than an oppression. Who will evoke the Antillean petty bourgeoisie with its racist complexes? That subtle appreciation of shades; that surface ease; the buried nostalgia of blue eyes; deeper in being, a certain reflex of vengeful contempt toward the "old white"; the mindless attachment to the Great Homeland (a symbol how vague and hollow ever since)... Tortured swarm of contradictions!... The most beautiful achievement of colonialism. It hasn't the tragic harshness of African forced labor, nor the splendor of executions by canon muzzles in the Indies, nor the flawless crispness of the razzias of the Far East, but how much more polished the work is! In truth, it is by their popular classes that colonial countries elude the internal gangrene of racism. I know that this no longer poses an immediate problem, but very much a secondary one, for the agricultural workers of the Antilles. But what to do when an "evolved" person from these countries, howbeit mutely populated with the noise of white superiority, and that I know to be neither imbecilic, nor radically uneducated, maintains that racism is an inevitable disposition, unstoppable, innate? Look at the result. That weighs as heavily in the balance of colonialism as do the executions, the exploitations and the famines. For in this first case, the enterprise has been wildly successful: the individual, beyond desperations and hatreds, has had the very measure of man torn from him. The racial problem is overtaken. (My heart burns from chewing nails!). I want to say that it must cease to be made into an absolute, to elucidate the driving reasons for racism, whether they are found to be social, economic or political, and which authorize it to continue to rage.

I had some idle time, the repose and the halt in experience that favor conclusions. A voyage. A "return to the sources;" the way one pulls on a stem to feel the resistance of the roots. I had cut the image in the mirror of the cities, I had reintegrated this manner of insidious peasantry, with a provincial air from the end of the world. Then I came back to France where eight years had maintained me in a disarray of new attractions.

And I had even better: these conflicts of every order (into misunderstandings between friends) which force you to retreat, which throw you into your silence, and behind the gun carriage of which you withdraw, stalking your intimate prey.

But the voyage only has sense inasmuch as the voyager knows what he is leaving and what he finds again. In keeping with whether he has been cut from his native land, by reason of profound ties he will have created for himself in the country of his exile; or on the contrary if he aspires to nothing so much as to return to his "zone of greater ease."

In truth, the answer here is double: because, wherever I go, I will feel solidarity with this "parcel of land" (not out of some sentimental regionalism, but because for me this land has slowly taken on the figure of a symbol — of a liberty to be gained, of an eminence to safeguard, which I attached to the ambition of a new sense of knowledge, a broadening and a conquest of the domains by all those present and to come — which means that the solidarity that I said is truly lived, in other words it is not a simple surge of affectivity, but also an element of culture); and on the other hand it is undeniable that a whole part of me, the most arid and the most friable in the same time, is here in Paris where I have known so many other faces of knowledge.

So, on the wool of noise, some object of silence rises, but so vast. It is for example the signal of morning, that comes and goes off on the milkman's cart. It is the bus that doesn't stop at this hour, and that I follow on its course: shooting star whose sound diminishes like the light of a long-gone comet. The man carries his movement toward the attentive windows; a street awakening has more reluctance than a cat. Who stops and contemplates? Here, thought organizes the exhibition of rags, and its charm lingers. There, giant cats scratch the earth, the steel of silence and objectless belief...

Yes, Paris once more. Place Furstenberg, which is one of the most melancholic decors of the world, seems to keep in the secret of its gas lamp a sort of answer that the city scatters all around. A single answer, when there are so many questions.

The smell of stones, the patience of the quais, the agitation of the train stations, the soup kitchens, the mind at the four burners, the black velvet of the snows, all night the ink of despair. Where is the answer, that the city buries in its surrounding neighborhoods?

Silence and solitude. The experience, to begin with, here, is that solitude does not elicit emotion; that it is understood with each handshake or snow. That it is necessary, on deferment of oblivion, to convince it, this solitude, to arm yourself against it. What asceticism, and what price. The atrocious rampart of voices cannot be underestimated. They fall. A wall of fogs. Who is friend? is not susceptible? artful? artful with virtue? artful with money? sensible to the future of his words? intelligent and subtle? subtle, and seeing coming? who has not prepared things? things? gazettes? bulletins? theories? sentences? who is not lucid? dialectician? artist? who hasn't got his author? his clan? where is art? — The truth that nonetheless alarms: poetry, knowledge, art are present. They ripen this universe, then grow from this multiplied solitude. They are, but yes, in this man who would sell you in order merely to occupy the space of ten pages of a journal; in this other, who flatters you, biding his time; in this third, a deaf-mute, whose lustrous cuff you shake. Yes, the friend who assures that. The other who applauds, but. I am only describing the circle, myself I am in it. Grandeur and servitude of Paris, that teaches the art of being alone. A hell without seasons. Out of which for each the Sun of Consciousness must rise.

SUN OF CONSCIOUSNESS

Several friends came by... They are here, under my gaze; we are here soon to be (it's a malediction) in search of the Proposition. All give themselves over to the exchange, but it is true that each reserves for himself an oasis, behind the words, where he consolidates. One lives in secret in the arena of a discussion. There are no longer individuals, but a single body tendered toward its destiny. At this level, I am not in the least insular, I do not represent; in this café I am a voice that adds itself to others. But like each I feel (whereas the brouhaha of propositions thickens, and here we are all tempting the fate of the real), that the residue in me remains; that it is true that literature cannot henceforth be the lodge of the soul; that this banal truth in its eternity, we will be several to have really suffered it; and behold, if possible, our chance. To impassion our logic, to measure our passions. Unprecedented opening of the world, and consciousness, crystallizing from this overture. Our most immediate power is beholden to this commonplace, which will have to be made into a reflexive harvest. Potency what's more of this city! that abstracts being, but to fling it straightaway into its very truth.

For we are, all, gathered on a single shore. The Atlantic that we must now cross, is the chaotic darkness that our very illuminations make. And here I am freezing between these two oceans; the true and immortal abyss of the sea, on the one hand, that exiles me from myself (from my reality, from my roots in the ground planted like so many pitchforks of truth); then the other, the enormous Wave besides that rolls here, Parisian. Knowing that these two Leviathans dissolve into one, that what denatures being is at the same time what opposes it to light, that the truth never departs from a very concrete bind, that it is made of a measure similar to those who seek, that it will be so for those who will have risked finding — that is what I am able to ensure that is most general, common, definitive, as to Experience.

And I protest that the matter is not in the details, that it is in the overview; in inventory perhaps of an amassment of remarks, but upon which diversity must be conducted to lead it toward a same detour. May the one whose language is solemn walk near the one whose speaking is concise. The splendor which, beyond the upheaval and threats of the modern world, assail the human spirit, is that of the discovery of the disparate, of the fundamental Other, who nourishes the nostalgia for unity. The epic of history entails this Movement.

The one who, at dawn, and while the fogs thicken the gesture, makes the first sign of friendship; he believes he is basking in the light of a fore-world, but that reveals a landscape of morning, in the still promised distance. Let him go, and attempt to fulfill that promise.

There is another sort of solidarity, more efficient. One can also say that the primary problem of our time is that of political choice. But I wish here only to follow the trace of my voyage, and not to propose lessons or programs. This manner of solidarity that I feel with regard to a friend, musician, essayist, actor or poet (myself having come from so far), it is perhaps not vain that in this place, after this long journey, and as though naturally (in the movement of Experience, one of its particulars), I signal it. So may it perhaps be possible to propose that a common search founds already common dimensions, after which each brings down his own walls. And is that not, if not a political task, then the work in progress of a more popular solidarity, then the very quotidian labor of a conviction, at least, with a very individual respect, like the sanction of a presence and the testimony of a total salutation? —What we may offer, is this: a continuous movement of literature, such that the movement is the strength and the weakness of a people, marching toward yet other lands.

I call generosity, not that loss of intelligence to the sentimentality that several of our literary censors seem to dread (folks who disentangle their petty minutiae), but on the contrary the attempt at reconquest of all the expanses of sensibility that were abandoned to the escalation of melodramas, of "classical" salons, or advertisements. This is perhaps where I find a larger purpose. For the bond seems natural to me between the absence of a collective dimension of the literary thing (a dimension that permits the enrichment of sensibility, founding it in knowledge) and these sorts of parties that are given in Paris, popular by name, in which the crowd (in couples, yes) frequents, without ever finding, itself. The literary minutia, even when lucid, foretells a disintegrated Body. Today, the general character of occidental art, what it shares among artists, is absence of community.

What the colonists and other possessors dispossessed of slaves have taken to calling in surface the exuberance and childishness of blacks is in depth this possibility of a collective sense, which polarizes individuals toward clear and most accessible forms (laughter, song, dance) of participation. Is that to say that this is a racially innate quality? Certainly not. I am saying only that this capacity has been dulled in the old West; that a total historical renewal is necessary for it to have another chance. Already, the assault French language and culture suffers on the part of those it has conquered throughout the world, obliges them to think themselves as a universal factor, one of the common places of the man who is exasperated toward his truth. (A reflection that often borrows, it is quite true, the imbecilic way of sneers or self-satisfaction).

In any case, regarding this capacity for consciousness, for collective participation (I do not say national), the weight of history is such, the possibility for innateness so null, that it has been possible to graft militarist gains, etc., on such a capital of collective communion ever since deformed, in order, under cover of historical conditions, to engender in a fraction of a people recognized among the most "artistic" of the world, the desolations of fascism. The elucidation of any collective force, of its mysteries and its ways, is a weapon against collective cataclysms. The very concrete knowledge of peoples, their popular consciousness, leads to the knowledge of the universal. But the universal no longer haunts us. So goes Unity, nourishing man.

View of the mind. Foam of the city, on the wave, unglimpsed. Whether on the wave, or in the city, the foam is fragile. It awaits its moment of being tried by the shore, and until then it struggles to endure on its crest. As for the ferryman of foams, what can he do in turn, if not endeavor to endure? Without even the certainty of the confrontation upon the shore. With only, between two breaths, the carried voice of those for him who are here proximate and unknown. Knowing then, at this time, that it is given to him, and for all reasons, to be both the same and the other, the son together and the stranger.

CITIES, POEMS

There are cities that are set against themselves, and lead you, from denial to denial, toward a certainty. Like Alexandria, city of clerics and scholars, before the great flame that was to burn its heart. I still imagine, in Athens the egoist, the barbarian ambler, tolerated by the citizen. The barbarian unknown to the Assemblies, that ostracism does not mark down, but who watches in secret the fall of swaths of the agora like the ruins of wonders. I imagine in the city, near those who are indifferent to the mission of their city, the stroll of the one who has come to find himself in this market where one loses one's way. Like Carthage again; but its vocation, faced with its mistress, Rome, made of this city a single warrior body, over which time passed too quickly. Assuredly, like those great capitals of Africa, in the time of splendor and courtesy. Too obscure cities, so slow, where the vine can slowly spread. Open cities, but so complex; they repel the blind whiteness of the new cities, the too delicate and seasonal enchantment of cities of art. They do not stir the gaze, except that one divines the multiple presence of the world. Open, not to the surface of countrysides and suburbs beyond their walls, but, like the Inca cities struck with desolations, to the altitude and the sky. They make a city-dweller of a villager, a city-dweller of an artist, a city-dweller of a man of the deserts. What is this magic? These cities affirm themselves at every turn of history, in these instants when everything is scattered and envenomed. So, they welcome the battered. They come to lose their way, they leave the muds of the earth, they unoccupy the concrete Great Voice, and lose themselves in the hive, where solitude fashions them. Then, they must regain the smear of the earth, the truth of the tree in front of the house. For the one who remains as for the one who leaves, there is then a taste of earth in the mouth, that fortifies the word. So Paris, at the heart of our time, receives, deracinates, blurs, then illumines and reassures. I know of a sudden its secret: and it is that Paris is an island, that intercepts from all sides and diffracts forthwith.

Presence and whole sovereignty of the world, as a space henceforth offered to the appetite, as a duration the full signification of which must be borne — whose mind can no longer depart from itself. Exoticism is very much dead, from the moment geography ceases to be absolute (in other words, here, limited to itself) to begin to have solidarity with its history which is man's. The confrontation of landscapes confirms that of cultures, sensibilities: not as the exaltation of an Unknown, but as that manner at last of being rid of one's skin to know one's projection in another light, the shadow of what one will be. The voyage is no longer premeditated, it is necessary. The immense pulverizing of discoveries, of analyses (from the exotic dream to the ethnographer's work through the book of adventures) has displaced the motives of sensibility. We may no longer dream of the secret cities of South America, without evoking the current condition of the peones; and we may no longer reflect upon the knowledge for which man has thirsted, without the terrestrial pulsation beating against us with its irremediable and tempting volley.

How desires are exacerbated then, and how difficult it is to preserve oneself against a sort of panic that exalts. It is the work of adolescence; and we are adolescent, in our new riches. Who hasn't dreamt of the poem that all things explains, of the philosophy whose last word illumines the universe, of the novel that organizes *all* the truths, all the passions, and conducts and enlightens them? An oeuvre that would begin upon the tranquil septentrional nights, unveiling each fjord, enflaming the Tropics, to calm itself in the white swaths of the South, a Novel that would furnish the liaisons, the intrications, the synthesis, the ONE?

Then, one must become closed to the flux. Or rather, listen carefully to it swell; but attach oneself at once to some square of earth, to problems of the everyday, to the strict measure of sight. Otherwise, we are submerged by our delirium, and the world vanishes in the smokes of the absolute disturbance itself has elicited. Art is indeed one of the domains of this fixation. Interested in one and then another chapter of the great moving book, and not the entire Swell, it emerges each time upon an attainment. And if it does not solve any problems, at least does it help also to pose them in the too diffuse light, when knowledge is possible and always future.

At last the muds have knotted the soul, filled it with solitudes;
And grounded their grasses when, raising its jungles from memory,
The road queries, with its shattered stones, with the wind!

It is not upon this face that the poet reads his crime,
Long since has his strength gone, long since
Has his flight left, upon all shores, iced this blood,
And is he tree of surface, forgetful of his depths,
Of the first blood, of the baptism — he is an abandoned storm...

(I had wearied the patience of the earth, I had known
How heavy is the sea after so much history, so much haymaking,
And shouted before her its apparition!)

Oh earth, oh better ennobled law, which is the book of abysses!
And from the crime of first falterings, to the centuries, swollen
The word! like a lane of flame trees, crying mercy.

March-April, 1955

A Note on the Translation

Sanglant et nu, de sang brûlé, nudité folle;
tandis que la mer se tait.[1]

ÉDOUARD GLISSANT, *Les Indes*

In an interview granted to French television in 1957, following the publication in 1956 of both *Soleil de la conscience* and the poetic work, *Les Indes*, Édouard Glissant identifies the snow as the propulsive force behind the writing of his first essay. Comparing the impression it sustains to that left by the flame trees of the Caribbean on European tourists of the day, he insists on the greater weight of the snow for an Antillean, for its permanence in French pedagogy, which imparts the seasons and a displaced geography to the students of what will soon become its overseas territories — derived from recent status as colonies. The snow holds in its essence the whole of the colonial enterprise as metonymy.

Édouard Glissant arrived from Martinique in Paris in 1946, where he was to study at the Sorbonne.[2] *Soleil de la conscience* is written from out of that displacement, and the reversals it operates needn't be belabored here, since they will find their way in the reader over the course of the text.

---

1. *Bloody and naked, of burnt blood, mad nakedness; whereas the sea falls silent.* —Tr. N.

2. At the time, only six bursaries were allocated to graduating students from all of Martinique to attend university in France, three in literature, three in the sciences. See Yves Billy and Mathieu Glissant, *Édouard Glissant, la créolisation du monde*, Production Auteurs associés, with the participation of France Télévisions, coll. "Empreintes," 2010.

1946[3] is a year marked in France's colonies by unwieldy postwar disappointment, and brutally subdued unrest (let the massacres at Sétif and Guelma in Algeria stand as fervent examples). Between 1941 and 1944, the island of Martinique, in the grip of a Vichy enterprise of exacerbated exploitation and unquenchable rapine, was stripped of its fruits for extradition to France, leaving large expanses of depleted land, and a hunger among the people, additionally isolated by the Allied blockades. Despite these embargoes, and against the powers of the seas, some 2,500 Martinicans joined the forces of Free France via the channels of Saint Lucia and Dominica (both under British rule) on small fishing craft. Many did not survive the initial journey, and those who did went on to the U.S. for training and eventual deployment in de Gaulle's service (largely in North Africa, but, uncannily, an Antillean contingent helped to liberate Bordeaux — one of France's important ports during the Atlantic slave trade[4]). These clandestine soldiers were known as *dissidents*,[5] a term of castigation flung at them by Admiral Georges Robert, Pétain's representative in Martinique; but it became an honorable epithet, serving to distinguish *dissidence* from *resistance*, a term reserved for European struggle against Hitlerism, and fascism more broadly speaking, but which didn't, by a reflexive turn, claim necessarily to undermine

---

3. 1946 marks the "official, if not real, end of a colonial system," and the transition, for Martinique and Guadeloupe, from colonies to the administrative status of overseas departments (département d'outre-mer). "It is the moment at which Martinicans as citizens send deputies to France." See Celia Britton and Édouard Glissant, "Souvenirs des années 40 à la Martinique: interview avec Édouard Glissant," in *L'Esprit créateur*, Vol. 47, No. 1, France's Colonies and the Second World War (Spring 2007), pp. 96-104.

4. Yves Billy and Mathieu Glissant, *op. cit.*

5. Among the *dissidents* was a young Frantz Fanon. See Éric T. Jennings, "La dissidence aux Antilles (1940-1943)," in *Vingtième Siècle. Revue d'histoire*, No. 68 (Oct.-Dec. 2000), p. 60.

colonialist assumptions.[6] This is made bloodily evident in the extension of slave labor conditions throughout the colonies, into the wars of de-colonization of the 1960's. (André Gide's *Voyage au Congo* is particularly eloquent in this regard.) Out of the sense of isolation and exasperation experienced during the war years in Martinique, Édouard Glissant will develop the concept of the *Tout-Monde* (all-world).[7]

But here, at the outset, with *Soleil de la conscience*, which inscribes in its matter poems from as early as 1948, the experience is still raw, and without explicit mention, is set against the assumptions of (French) universalism, and inscription of distancing, situation, and emplacement. As Glissant will write in *L'intention poétique*, the essay that follows *Soleil de la conscience*: "You say: *overseas* (we said it with you), but you too will soon be overseas."[8]

---

6. This distinction is borne out in a post-war decision by the French Ministry of the Colonies to distance French resistants from Antillean resistants who were perceived to pose a threat to French unity through eventual separatist claims. "The departmentalization of the Antilles in 1946 was in fact itself justified as a measure destined to 'cut short all foreign covetousness.'" See Éric T. Jennings, op. cit., p. 71. Also Éliane Sempaire, *La dissidence an tan Sorin (1940-1943) « au nom de la patrie »*. Pointe-à-Pitre, Éditions Jasor, 1988, p. 17. At the liberation of Paris in 1944, under compliance with orders from the U.S. government the French military under De Gaulle undertook to "whitewash" its troops, ensuring that only white soldiers were to march into Paris, stripping black soldiers of their uniforms and extending them to inexperienced white surrogates. While the motivations for *dissidence* were numerous, and not always for reasons of French liberation, there was, and continues to be, a near-unanimous sentiment of refusal among surviving *dissidents*, unrecognized for more than sixty years, to repeat their acts were such a situation to present itself again. Certainly, their experience in Vietnam confirmed this. See, for example, *Le blanchiment des troupes coloniales* (dir. Jean-Baptiste Dusséaux, 2015); *Parcours de dissidents* (dir. Euzhan Palcy, 2006) and *Héritiers du Vietnam* (dir. Arlette Pacquit, 2015).

7. Édouard Glissant, *Tout-Monde*. Paris: Gallimard, 1993; *Traité du tout-monde (Poétique IV)*. Paris: Gallimard, 1997.

8. *Poetic Intention*, tr. Nathanaël, with Anne Malena. New York: Nightboat Books, 2010, p. 16.

The French word *conscience* provides a difficult vantage for English, for it is split along a dual sense, of both *consciousness* and *conscience*. Each encounter with the word in translation requires the recollection of this particular emphasis, with an additional attention given to *awareness*. Such that *Sun of Consciousness* is an ethic, as well as a form of attentiveness, an awakening to itself, and to the world, that demands the same in return. It is also the call to memory from out of a lost history.[9] Here, what will be deployed throughout Glissant's oeuvre as exfoliations of *l'un* (the one) — *l'unique, l'unité, univers*, etc. — ask to be read *against* universalism, which is at the pernicious root of French cultural expansionism and colonial exploitation and enslavement:

> *The city is all the more secret that you offer yourself to its secret; the Measure will be the same for all; yet whosoever seeks unity first crystalizes it in his own language.*

Indeed,

> The very concrete knowledge of peoples, their popular consciousness, leads to the knowledge of the universal. But the universal no longer haunts us. So goes Unity, nourishing man.

Soleil de la conscience, while a deceptively small volume, is epic in proportion. It asks to be read in keeping with a vast time signature, detailed, and slow, and if I have been obstinate in my insistence upon Glissant's seemingly idiosyncratic punctuation, it is because so much of his thinking resides there.

---

9. "The history of Martinique is a lost history: obliterated in the collective consciousness (memory) by the concerted act of the colonizer." Édouard Glissant. *Le Discours antillais*. Paris: Gallimard, 1997 [Seuil: 1981], p. 185.

In *Le Discours antillais*,[10] Glissant defends what he refers to as "the baroque insolence of language." He identifies the "colonial baroque" as a "response to an unconsciously felt lack." And while it is accordingly visible *on site* in the architecture of Latin America, "the Antillean baroque is not carried by works [*œuvres*] but by language." Here, English cannot render a proper distinction between *langage*, the term employed in the text, and langue, which English construes with indistinction.[11] "The baroque colonial in the French Antilles is literary." Glissant further qualifies this as "the flamboyance of a vacuum." And already, this sentence, in French, *la flamboyance d'un vide*, is a translation in itself, replete with organic resonances, and transposed specificity — the flamboyant is the flame tree, and despite its literary register appealing to brilliancy, it is also suggestive of a vacuum or emptiness having turned to "sheets of fire."

In this translation, I have avoided commentary within the text. As such, the reader will not find indication in the form of bracketed recall, of each instance, for example, of the word *connaissance*, whose polysemy provides healthy doses of disorientation, since it can range in meaning from the word *knowledge* (which also, incidentally, translates the French word *savoir*) to *an acquaintance*. In defense of a poetics of the work, and its fragile cadence, in addition to the inevitable displacements it will suffer in its transposition to English, I assume responsibility for every departure of sense. So, each time, the word *Surge* surfaces in the text, the French *Élan* will only be intimated, untranslatable such as it is. As in *Poetic Intention*, I have continued to render *errance* as *errance*, preferring to avoid the heavily connoted term *errantry* often

10. *Ibid.* Page 128 for the passages that follow.
11. "Language [*la langue*] creates the rapport, language [*le langage*] creates the difference, one and other each as precious." *Ibid.*, p. 552.

used as corollary (when reading across volumes, translations and translators, this active discrepancy ought to be kept in mind).

To the creatures of this text, I confide the secret of their name. This work is a tender geography, holding still very close what will emerge suffuse and generously proliferate throughout the author's oeuvre. "What can writing do? It never catches up."[12] I wish to acknowledge for their friendship and counsel at points of particular consternation, the inexhaustive generosity of Catherine Mavrikakis, Hervé Sanson, Jennifer Scappettone, Sylvie Glissant, Myriam Suchet, and for his patient remarks on the English text, Nathaniel Feis. To Bilal Hashmi, I am ever indebted for his editorial acumen and his careful eye on my work.

And finally, to Sylvie, once more, my most replete gratitude for her unyielding confidence.

Nathanaël
August 25, 2019

---

12 *Ibid.*, p. 20.

ÉDOUARD GLISSANT (1928-2011) introduced the notion of *antillanité* as a way of reconsidering the world as archipelago. A thinker of the creolization of cultures and the poetics of relation, his multi-faceted œuvre moves between the essay (*Faulkner, Mississippi*), poetry (*The Indies*), fiction (*The Fourth Century*) and theatre (*Monsieur Toussaint*). In 1958, he was awarded the Prix Renaudot for *The Ripening*. Édouard Glissant taught in the United States at Louisiana State University and at the City University in New York. In 2006, he founded the Institut du Tout-Monde in Paris.

NATHANAËL is the author of more than thirty books written in French or in English and published in the United States, Québec and France. Her translations include works by Édouard Glissant, Catherine Mavrikakis, Hervé Guibert, and Hilda Hilst (the latter in collaboration with Rachel Gontijo Araújo).

Works by Édouard Glissant in English translation

Fiction

1958: *The Ripening*, tr. Frances Frenaye. New York: George Braziller, 1959.
1964: *The Fourth Century*, tr. Betsy Wing. Lincoln: University of Nebraska Press, 2001.
1981: *The Overseer's Cabin*, tr. Betsy Wing. Lincoln: University of Nebraska Press, 2011.

Poetry

1956: *The Indies / Les Indes*, tr. Dominique O'Neill. Toronto: GREF, 1992.
1960: *Black Salt: Poems*, tr. Betsy Wing. Ann Arbor: University of Michigan Press, 1998.
1994: *Complete Poetry*, tr. Jeff Humphries and Melissa Manolas. Minneapolis: University of Minnesota Press, 2005.

Essays

1956: *Sun of Consciousness*, tr. Nathanaël. New York: Nightboat Books, 2020.
1959: *Poetic Intention*, tr. Nathanaël. New York: Nightboat Books, 2010.
1981: *Caribbean Discourse: Selected Essays*, tr. Michael Dash. Charlottesville: University Press, of Virginia, 1989.
1990: *Poetics of Relation*, tr. Betsy Wing. Ann Arbor: Michigan University Press, 1997.
1996: *Faulkner, Mississippi*, tr. Barbara B. Lewis and Thomas C. Spear. New York: Farrar, Straus and Giroux, 1999.
1996: *Introduction to a Poetics of Diversity*, tr. Celia Britton. Liverpool: Liverpool University Press, 2020.
1997: *Treatise on the Whole-World*, tr. Celia Britton. Liverpool: Liverpool University Press, 2020.

Theatre

1986: *Monsieur Toussaint*, tr. Joseph G. Foster and Barbara A. Franklin. Washington: Three Continents Press, 1981; tr. Michael Dash. Boulder: Lynne Rienner Publishers, 2005.

NIGHTBOAT BOOKS

Nightboat Books, a nonprofit organization, seeks to develop audiences for writers whose work resists convention and transcends boundaries. We publish books rich with poignancy, intelligence, and risk. Please visit nightboat.org to learn about our titles and how you can support our future publications.

The following individuals have supported the publication of this book. We thank them for their generosity and commitment to the mission of Nightboat Books:

Kazim Ali
Anonymous
Jean C. Ballantyne
Photios Giovanis
Amanda Greenberger
Elizabeth Motika
Benjamin Taylor
Peter Waldor
Jerrie Whitfield & Richard Motika

Nightboat Books gratefully acknowledges support from the National Endowment for the Arts.